ABC

Americana

from the

NATIONAL GALLERY OF ART

SELECTED BY

Cynthia Elyce Rubin

Gulliver Books

Harcourt Brace Jovanovich, Publishers

San Diego   New York   London

Library of Congress Cataloging-in-Publication Data
Rubin, Cynthia Elyce.
ABC Americana from the National Gallery of Art/selected by
Cynthia Elyce Rubin; [photographs by Carleton Palmer].—1st ed.
p.   cm.
"Gulliver books."
Summary: Presents, in alphabetical order, a selection of twenty-six watercolor
paintings from the Index of American Design, a graphic archive
of American folk and decorative arts.
ISBN 0-15-200660-5
1. Americana—Catalogs—Juvenile literature. 2. Decorative arts—
United States—Catalogs—Juvenile literature. 3. English language—
Alphabet—Juvenile literature. 4. National Gallery of Art—
Catalogs—Juvenile literature. [1. Americana—Catalogs.
2. Decorative arts. 3. National Gallery of Art. 4. Alphabet.]
I. Palmer, Carleton, ill. II. National Gallery of Art. (U.S.)
III. Index of American Design. IV. Title.
NK805.R8   1989
745′.0973—dc19   88-17740

First edition   A B C D E

The display type was set in Caslon 471 by Latent Lettering, New York, New York.
The text type was set in Caslon by Thompson Type, San Diego, California.
Printed and bound by Tien Wah Press, Singapore
Production supervision by Warren Wallerstein and Eileen McGlone
Designed by G. B. D. Smith

Preface

The source of the remarkable artwork in this ABC is the Index of American Design, a graphic archive of American decorative arts from the colonial period through the nineteenth century. The Index was conceived during the Depression as a federal work project for artists to create in watercolors a visual record of representative objects of American design and folk art. The result — produced between 1935 and 1942 — is a collection of nearly seventeen thousand paintings, all of which the National Gallery of Art acquired in 1943. Since then, the Index paintings have been made accessible in books, microfiche sets, slide programs, and exhibitions throughout the country. In its ongoing effort to share the treasures of the Index, the National Gallery of Art presents here twenty-six of its most vivid and meticulously detailed renderings, specially selected to stimulate the eyes and minds of young children. All ages, however, will find visual delight in this book.

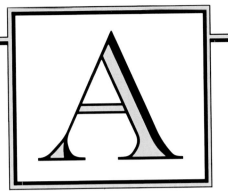

is for Angel

B

is for Boot

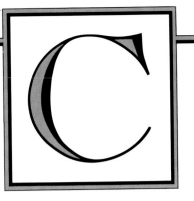

is for Circus wagon

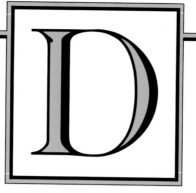

is for Drum

E

is for Elephant

F

is for Figurehead

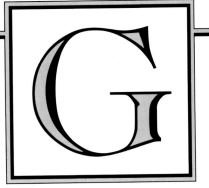

G

is for Glasses

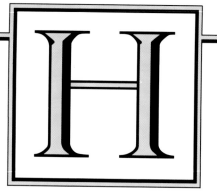

is for Horse

is for Indian

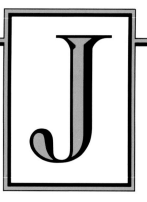

is for Jug

K

is for Key

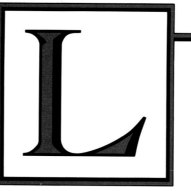

is for Lumberjacks

is for Marionette

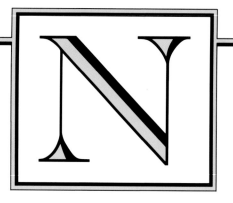

is for Nutcracker

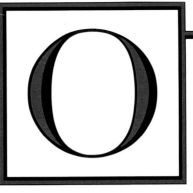

O

is for Oxen

is for Pig

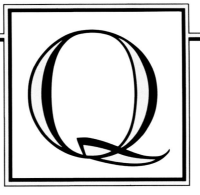

is for Quilt

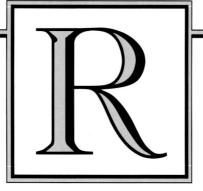

is for Roosters

is for Saddle

T

is for Trumpet

is for Uncle Sam

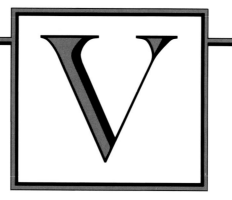

is for Valentine

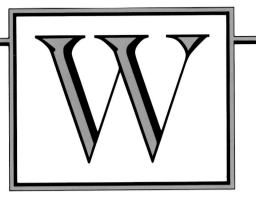

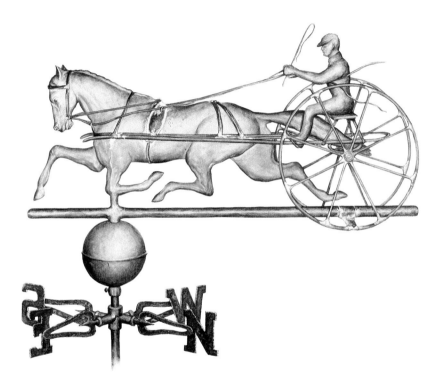

is for Weather vane

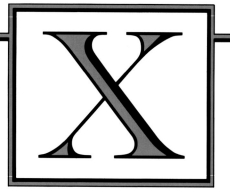

is for X *pattern*

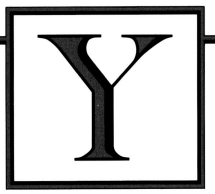

ESTATE OF JOHN APPLEYARD IN THE YEAR 1851. WORKED IN 1907.

is for Yard

Z

is for **Zigzag**

A is for Angel
Copper *Angel Gabriel* weather vane
Artist: Harriette Gale

B is for Boot
Wood shop sign
Artist: Albert Ryder

C is for Circus wagon
Wood circus wagon from Barnum and Bailey Circus
Artist: Howard R. Weld

D is for Drum
Painted wood Civil War drum
Artist: Wayne White

E is for Elephant
Painted cast-iron toy bank
Artist: Frank Gray

F is for Figurehead
Oak figurehead
Artist: Elizabeth Moutal

G is for Glasses
Gilded zinc and iron shop sign
Artist: John Tercuzzi

H is for Horse
Carved and painted pine toy horse
Artist: Mina Lowry

I is for Indian
Cast-metal display Indian
Artist: Walter Hochstrasser

J is for Jug
Salt-glazed stoneware jug
Artist: Nicholas Amantea

K is for Key
Painted pine shop sign
Artist: Henry Tomaszewski

L is for Lumberjacks
Carved wood lumberjacks
Artist: Frank Eiseman

M is for Marionette
Carved and painted walnut juggling marionette
Artist: Elmer Weise

N is for Nutcracker
Painted wood nutcracker
Artist: Virginia T. Richards

O is for Oxen
Carved pine miniature oxen and oxcart
Artist: Eugene Bartz

P is for Pig
Painted pine butcher shop sign
Artist: Laura Bilodeau

Q is for Quilt
Silk star and flag pattern quilt
Artist: Fred Hassebrock

R is for Roosters
Embroidered wool rug
Artist: Dorothy Lacey

S is for Saddle
Leather saddle with iron stirrups
Artist: Bertha Semple

T is for Trumpet
Engraved silver fireman's speaking trumpet
Artist: Samuel O. Klein

U is for Uncle Sam
Painted cast-iron toy bank
Artist: Kurt Melzer

V is for Valentine
Cut and painted paper valentine
Artist: John Thorsen

W is for Weather vane
Copper and iron weather vane
Artist: Samuel W. Ford

X is for X pattern
Cotton quilt
Artist: Edith M. Magnette

Y is for Yard
Silk yarn picture on perforated paper
Artist: Edward Unger

Z is for Zigzag
Silk and wool petitpoint handbag
Artist: Herbert Marsh